THINK
LIKE A
MANAGER
DON'T
ACT LIKE
ONE

For Charlotte Starren and Bas Faase

THINK LIKE A MANAGER

DON'T ACT LIKE ONE

75 approaches

HARRY STARREN

BIS Publishers
Building 'Het Sieraad'
Postjesweg 1
1057 DT Amsterdam, The Netherlands
T +31 (0)20 515 02 30
bis@bispublishers.com
www.bispublishers.com

ISBN 978 90 6369 347 3

Copyright © 2016

Text: Harry Starren
Concept: Aernoud Bourdrez
Concept and realisation: buro van Ons
DTP: Guus de Graaf
Portrait Harry Starren: Muriel Janssen

For questions: info@harrystarren.com

INTRODUCTION

Managers, we all know them. They make sure that things get done, that agreements are observed and that results are achieved. Ten years ago they were seen as the ideal solution for many companies. These days, their very existence is being called into question. Why this separate role? After all, managing is something we all do. That is why I've written Think Like a Manager, Don't Act Like One.

In this collection – you can't really call it a book – I explain how to do just that. By acting in a different way, or sometimes by not acting at all. By listening rather than talking. By letting others have their own way, instead of always getting yours. A manager (a) does the right things, (b) does them well, (c) works with others, and (d) looks to the future. This collection is presented in that same order, in the form of a series of observations – my own and other people's. I offer them to you as food for thought.

For example, I show you how – like Alexander Fleming – you can find something of inestimable value by not looking for it. What the moon landing of 1969 teaches us about setting goals. Why you should never motivate professional employees. And that timing is everything.

This collection may well irritate you from time to time, and possibly inspire you, but really it should make you think. It probably wouldn't be sensible to follow every one of my suggestions, but they might give you some fresh ideas. Because those who keep doing what they've always done only achieve the results they've always achieved.

Harry Starren

CONTENT

DO THE RIGHT THINGS

DO THEM WELL

WORK WITH OTHERS

LOOK TO THE FUTURE

INNOVATION IN MODERATION

Making a success of something entirely new is harder now than it has ever been. A novelty that builds on what's already there is far more likely to be accepted, because it's known and trusted. Dessert manufacturers understand this principle better than anyone. Custard has been the same for years, but now it's "organic", "with a dash of chocolate", or "sugar-free!".

THE CUSTOMER IS YOUR GUIDE

Anyone who pays close attention when they install a software update is likely to make a remarkable discovery. Many of the new functions and features aren't innovations by the designer, but improvements suggested by users. The program is suddenly capable of more than the original maker could ever have imagined. Sometimes you need your customer's eyes to reveal the real potential of a product.

THE UNEXPECTED DISCOVERY

In the world of literature we call it serendipity: the unexpected discovery. Think of it like a visit to a flea market. You're not really looking for anything, but then suddenly, there among all the junk, you find that thing you always wanted. In science and technology, such discoveries are surprisingly common. While he was tidying up his laboratory, Alexander Fleming came across a mold that had settled on a Petri dish culturing colonies of Staphylococcus bacteria. Around the mold he saw an area free of bacteria. He went on to isolate the substance being produced by the mold and so discovered penicillin. Sometimes you have to look for nothing in order to find something. ■

THOSE WHO FALL PREY TO SMALL TEMPTATIONS DON'T DESERVE BIG ONES

And those who fall prey to big temptations lose everything in the end.

■

THE VALLEY IS THE GOAL

In his legendary and much-quoted 1961 speech to Congress, President John F. Kennedy declared, "I believe that this nation should commit itself to achieving the goal, before this decade is out, of landing a man on the moon..." But the most interesting thing is how he ended the sentence: "and returning him safely to the Earth." Every climber recognizes that sentiment. The goal is not the summit. That's just an ecstatic stop on the way. The real challenge is making it back down again in one piece. Think beyond the apparent objective and set your sights on the valley, because the greatest dangers await you on your return journey. Just look at Odysseus. ■

STROKING A TIGER DOESN'T MAKE IT A CAT

In a zoo, a lamb is peacefully sharing a cage with a lion.
"How did you manage that?", asks a surprised visitor.
"Three lambs a day," answers the keeper. A natural enemy
is never placated – it has to be beaten or avoided.

#7

ENVY IS THE WRITING ON THE WALL

Envy. In general, a negative quality and one we learn to suppress in ourselves and to deny when challenged about it. Envy isn't pretty. Yet sometimes it's a good guide to long-cherished desires. What we envy in others can point the way to our own happiness. Envy says more than you think – as does indifference. ■

DO WHAT'S POSSIBLE, NOT WHAT'S PERMISSIBLE

At one time it was enough to get you fired from a university. Ten years ago, as a professor you were banned from owning your company, practicing your profession independently or even setting up a charitable foundation. Nowadays, the job ads say that professors are expected to possess demonstrable commercial ability. Owning a business has suddenly become an advantage in getting hired. Or take employment agencies. In the Netherlands they were illegal until Frits Goldschmeding set up Amstelveen. After much resistance, it was finally legalized, started spreading its wings, and was renamed Randstad. Today it's a global concern. ■

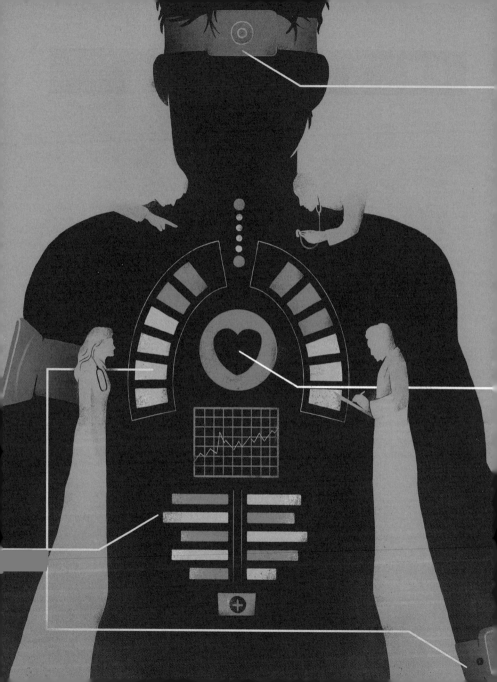

BREAK-THROUGHS COME FROM OUTSIDE

The greatest advances in public healthcare have been made not by doctors, but by engineers. In the nineteenth century they built water mains and brought us modern sewers. As they did so, average life expectancy increased by leap and bounds. The breakthroughs came from outside. And they still do. There's evidence that adolescents' performance in school improves immensely if they start later in the day, get more exercise during classes and work in cool surroundings. No teacher can argue with the science. For real innovation, outsiders are in the best place.

THREE WAYS TO REACH YOUR TARGET

There are three ways to reach a target. If you know where you are and where you want to go, just take the direct route. Making sure that you formulate clear and measurable goals. Management professional Peter Drucker calls this "management by objectives" and he considers it best suited for trivial goals. With more strategic ones, the direction you take is more important than the goal itself. What are the obstacles along the way, and what options do you have? The third way sounds like cheating: you only define your goal once you've reached it. That way, you always succeed. While you may think this is easy, in fact it merits a lesson of its own... ■

SET YOUR GOAL ONCE YOU'VE HIT IT

Two boys were standing by a pond, taking turns throwing stones. After a while, one of them started shouting "Hit!" after each throw. Once I'd seen this a few times, I suddenly realized what was happening. The boy had only set his target after he'd first hit it several times. From then on, that was what he did every time. Every throw was a hit. Defining your target in advance is the conventional approach, and not a bad one, but it does have its drawbacks. For a start, you can end up staring blindly into the future, at your goal, and so forget that you've already achieved something. Sometimes you've even achieved the goal itself, without even noticing. ■

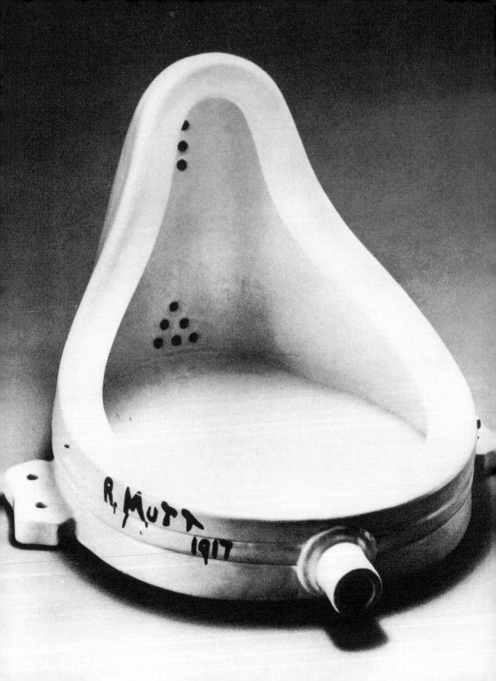

DISCOVER YOUR STRATEGY

The Danish philosopher Søren Kierkegaard once said, "Life can only be understood backwards; but it must be lived forwards." In other words, you only know what you're doing once you've done it. That's why it's a good idea for companies to call the occasional time out, in order to discover the patterns in their own operations. This often gives them a better grip on the strategy they're actually following. The manager's role here is to reinforce what's already being done well. Sometimes, good management is about lagging behind. ∎

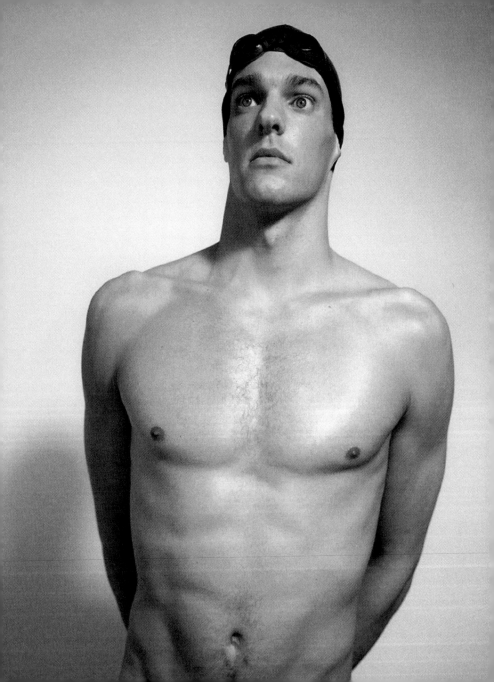

 # 13

BE THE ALTERNATIVE

In business, it's considered a matter of faith: there's always room for an alternative provider. When I was director of a postgraduate school of Business Administration, we introduced a Master's degree program for public-sector managers. There was already a similar but far more expensive course, so we were offering the affordable alternative. And when that expensive course closed, we celebrated. In our eyes, we'd "won". But we soon started losing business, too. That's because we were no longer the affordable alternative, but for many potential customers had become a "vastly overpriced" monopoly.

THERE ARE NO FACTS

The German philosopher Friedrich Nietzsche said, "There are no facts, only interpretations." The truth lies not in things themselves, but in how you look at them. In one newspaper an athlete wins silver, in another she loses out on gold. The same goes for organizations. Do you say a startup's initial losses are because it's investing in the future, or because it launched with the wrong financial policy? ■

## 15

CREATE NEW COMBI- NATIONS

According to the Austrian-American economist Joseph Schumpeter, entrepreneurship generates economic dynamism. Entrepreneurs create new combinations and so render old ones obsolete. Schumpeter coined the term "creative destruction" to describe this process: the good making way for the better, with economic progress as the result. Every good creation destroys a not-so-good one. Just as Uber is revolutionizing the taxi industry. And historic buildings are saved by finding new uses for them.

## 16

SAME SAME BUT DIFFERENT

Small innovations can have major consequences.
"Same same but different" is a property the market finds easy
to understand. Especially when that "different" is also better.
To launch a whole new idea successfully, it helps to have a
metaphor people are already familiar with. The car as a horseless
carriage. The fax as a telex, but different. The Walkman as
a cassette player for music, but in a truly portable form.

## 17

BE
MODERATE

The "golden mean", the Aristotelian middle way, has become a more or less universal doctrine. By imagining the two extremes in any decision we make, then choosing the point half-way between them, we tread the path of moderation. Centralization or decentralization? Autocracy or participation? The ideal always seems to be somewhere in the middle, but finding it requires the ability to philosophize. A skill that Aristotle acquired from Socrates. ■

## 18

IF YOU CAN'T DO IT THE WAY IT SHOULD BE DONE, DO IT THE WAY IT CAN BE DONE

We can all start something, but the point is to finish it. Perseverance is a vital trait for entrepreneurs. That may seem at odds with flexibility, but really it's all about the art of the possible. And, if something does prove impossible, having the courage to decide to do something else. The Dutch politician Jan de Koning used to say, "If you can't do it the way it should be done, do it the way it can be done." Stubbornly pursuing the impossible may show determination, but true perseverance lies in seeking another path. ∎

## 19

TIME MAKES THE DIFFERENCE

The Chinese military strategist Sun Tzu called time the most important weapon in warfare. Take Napoleon Bonaparte, who used it to his advantage by always – well, almost always – moving faster than his enemies. That was until Waterloo, where lack of time proved his downfall. Speed is the key to business success, except when the opposite applies. Sometimes, having more time than the rest can pay dividends. Whatever the case, time makes the difference. ■

## 20

FAIL
FASTER

You can only succeed if you're willing to fail. That's the price you have to pay for success. Who remembers the Apple Newton, the hand-held computer that was supposed to change the world? Or any number of unsuccessful TV formats? The faster you fail, the faster you can come up with something better. Unilever pulls a lot of its latest product innovations off the shelves almost before you realize they're there. And my publisher's list certainly consists of more than a few fast-selling titles. Perhaps the real key to success is failing faster than the rest. ■

DON'T KNOW TILL YOU DO

It's tempting to want to know it all, right now, but it's far more sensible to wait until you really know. Good doctors take their time to reach a diagnosis, as do judges with their verdicts. Once you've made your decision, tunnel vision can set in. On the night of the 1948 US presidential election, the Chicago Daily Tribune, persuaded by polls and conventional wisdom, went to press early with the headline "Dewey Defeats Truman". By the next morning, it was clear that Truman had won.

22

AMBITIOUS GOALS MAKE MODEST ONES ACHIEVABLE

"We're the pole – you decide where you set the bar."
That's the slogan of a well-known Dutch distance learning college, in a commercial featuring a pole vaulter. The biggest obstacle you face in life is yourself. But it helps if you set yourself ambitious goals. No, fantastic ones. A karate practitioner learning to break a plank with his bare hand is taught to aim for a point beyond it. This makes the plank itself easier to break – it becomes nothing more than an obstacle on the route to the final objective. ∎

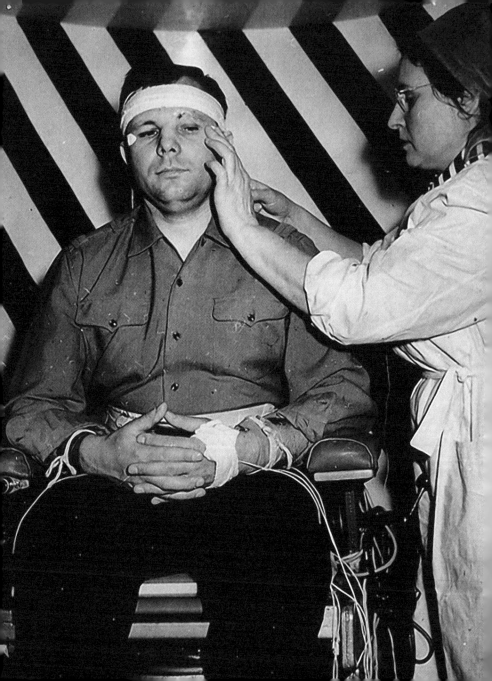

START BY LOOKING BACK

Or, to quote the first line of Stephen Covey's famous book, The Seven Habits of Highly Effective People, "Begin with the End in Mind". From there, work your way back to where you are now. Coming from the opposite direction, obstacles that seem insurmountable from the other side are easily avoided. A lot of wasted effort need not be regretted, and much of what we do doesn't help us to achieve our goal. Only those who keep that final objective in mind can be fruitfully efficient, since effectiveness – especially – comes before efficiency. The question always remains the same: what do you want to achieve? ∎

## 24

LEAP BEFORE YOU LOOK

As Isaac Newton discovered centuries ago, it's easier to guide what's already in motion than to get a motionless object to move in any direction. That takes much more energy.
A lot of operations bog down in well-intentioned proposals or endless reflection. It's easier and more effective to get things moving first, then make the adjustments needed to reach your objective. Start, and only then write a business plan.

REPEAT IT LIKE IT'S THE FIRST TIME

First and foremost, leadership is about creating joy in the repetition of what you've already said. Every actor knows that, and so does every president. Barack Obama's "Yes We Can" campaign spread through America like a gospel. Leadership is a performing art. ■

FORM CREATES CONTENT

During the Northern Ireland peace process, even the shape of the negotiating table proved controversial. Former British Prime Minister Tony Blair recalls that the Unionists wanted the two sides to face each other as adversaries, while the Republicans wanted them to sit next to each other as partners. The impasse was only broken when an official suggested a diamond-shaped table, so that they could sit both opposite and with each other. ■

27

THE TEST
OF A
FIRST RATE
INTELLIGENCE
IS THE
ABILITY
TO HOLD
TWO OPPOSED
IDEAS IN MIND
AT THE SAME
TIME AND STILL
RETAIN
THE ABILITY
TO FUNCTION

F. Scott Fitzgerald*

*In The Great Gatsby. ■

THINK LIKE A MANAGER DON'T ACT LIKE ONE

HARRY STARREN

## 28

DON'T READ BESTSELLERS
(the rest already do)

Bestsellers are read by a lot of people. That's what makes a book a bestseller. Nothing wrong with that, you might think, but it also makes their contents common knowledge. To learn more, and to learn different things, you're better off drawing on other sources. That keeps you distinctive. Whatever great insights the bestsellers have to offer will reach you anyway. ■

DON'T DO IT

Organizations are action-driven. Managers are supposed to be decisive. Nobody talks about the importance of silence, and we continue to underestimate the power of doing nothing. Inaction is not always as bad as it seems. Grass doesn't grow faster if you tug at it.

BURNING CHICKENS

Apparently, the best way to burn down a building and hide the cause is to douse live chickens with gasoline and set them alight. In their panic, the birds run in all directions and start new fires everywhere. If you want everyone in an organization to know something, then you need burning chickens. Nobody knows where the fire came from, but in no time they're all ablaze.

## 31

HE WHO SOWS ORDER WILL REAP CHAOS

This is the title of Walter Baets' book on Chaos Theory.
It teaches us that, sooner or later, chaos always passes through
a moment of order. Just give it time. Take a busy urban road
junction in Thailand, with not a traffic light in sight. After a while,
a pattern emerges which is able to cope with three times as
much traffic as our light-controlled cities. When the local authority
in Drachten, a village in the north of the Netherlands, removed
all the road signs, it actually cut the number of accidents. ■

## 32

CIRCULAR THINKING

There are three types of logic. The first is the linear logic you start learning at elementary school – the logic of cause and effect, question and answer, problem and solution. Clear-cut, black and white. Then you learn that one effect can have multiple causes, and one cause multiple effects. You could call this a plural logic that helps us understand complex situations. Finally, there's circular logic, the relational form in which cause becomes effect and effect becomes cause. The chicken and the egg. Services are always relational in nature, and so benefit from mastery of this third form. Just as good students make their teachers better. And a good audience makes for a better performance. ■

## 33

POSTPONE YOUR JUDGMENT

To learn, put off passing judgment. Judgmental people are the most obstinate kind, because a judgment is an opinion that precludes further learning. Certainty impedes discovery, and being 100% certain closes all roads to new insights. Right? Maybe, but how can I know for sure?

■

EVERY DISADVANTAGE HAS ITS ADVANTAGE

That was the late, great soccer star Johan Cruijff's way of saying "Every cloud has a silver lining". When one of his players was sent off, Cruijff pointed out that having just ten men on the field made it easier to decide who to pass to. This typifies his ability to see the other side of the coin. One person's disaster is another's opportunity.

POLICE DEPT.
JACKSON, MISS
20897
3-2980

## 35

EVERY ADVANTAGE HAS ITS DISADVANTAGE

Someone once said that truths that can be twisted so much they become true again are deeper truths. Where you stand depends on where you sit. When someone in the village where I was born complained about the rain, there was always someone else who'd say, "But it's good for the farmers". The greater your reputation, the more you have to lose. And the less room for maneuver that leaves you. An aristocratic title brings privileges, it also means you're expected to behave in a certain way: noblesse oblige. ■

## 36

THINKING
IS
DOING

"There is nothing as practical as a good theory," said Kurt Lewin. If something doesn't work, that's usually because it's based on a false assumption. A flawed theory. The word "theory" derives from Greek and means something like "observation". So a theoretician is someone who's good at observing. Steve Jobs called innovation a question of looking carefully. Finding a good theory is important, because nothing is as impractical as a bad one. If the theory's right, then the practice will work of its own accord. As Auguste Rodin once said, "Sculpture is easy: I choose a block of marble and chop off whatever I don't need." ■

## 37

DETACHED INVOLVEMENT

It can be great to immerse yourself completely in something. To lose yourself in it. But what exactly are you losing? Managers who view their work as a game are generally more effective than those who treat it as hard reality. The Indian management guru Jagdish Parikh urges us to adopt "detached involvement" as our professional attitude to life. A paradoxical stance: despite feeling deeply engaged with your work, you have to be able to distance yourself from it. Just as a painter steps back from the canvas to avoid losing himself in it. ■

## 38

TIMING
IS
EVERYTHING

Timing is crucial in every profession. It's what makes the difference. Frank Sinatra had a wonderful voice, but it was his timing that made him unique. The same with Billy Holliday and Ella Fitzgerald. And in sports, too, but also in successful business negotiations and good meetings. The right word at the right moment. The well-timed joke that raises a laugh, rather than the badly timed one that leaves everyone cold. Good timing is best learnt by watching and listening carefully. It's a practical skill. ■

## 39

SAY YES TO PRINCIPLES, NO TO RULES

A person with principles can live without rules. Look at the roads. Traffic lights and road signs represent rules. But "Slow vehicles take priority over fast vehicles" is a principle, not a rule. Just as the roundabout embodies a principle. That is, traffic already on it has right of way. If there's none there, you can enter the circle unhindered. No prescriptive measure can beat this adaptive arrangement. How often have you stood at a red light with no other traffic in sight? ■

## 40

IMITATE NATURE

The most important factor in our current economic development is technological progress. Yet even that is often rooted in nature. It's there that we discover solutions we could never find with human endeavor alone. It's the source of our medicines, our energy, and the chemicals making up the products all around us. Nature shows us the way. We sometimes need only to imitate her in order to understand the world better. ■

CASANOVA WAS A LISTENER

Persuasion relies on the gift of eloquence. To make a real connection, though, you need the ability to listen. Casanova understood that better than anyone. Sure, he could talk. But his real skill was listening. That made him irresistible. ∎

GIVE IN TO GET WHAT YOU WANT

Ernst Happel, a celebrated Austrian soccer coach, was appointed trainer of a Dutch team. At his first training session, he asked the squad, "What do you want?" An unexpected question for star players used to authoritarian coaches. "A game", they replied. So Happel rolled a ball onto the pitch. The players had their game. A little later he rolled in a second ball, and a couple of minutes after that a third. The game had suddenly become a training session again. With balls coming at them from all directions, the players had to put in all their effort. Mentally as well as physically. After fifteen minutes they were forced to give up, exhausted. Happel just smiled. He'd given them want they wanted, but it was his choice of game. ■

## 43

CHANGE HAPPENS OF ITS OWN ACCORD

Change is often regarded as a tough process. That's an idea managers benefit from: it makes their task difficult, and so ensures that they're well paid. Actually, though, people don't find it that hard to change – it's in our nature. We adapt to circumstances. Fear of change is a myth, as Professor Hans Wissema has discovered. But people want to change themselves, they don't want to be changed by others.

#44

THE BENEFITS OF ILLNESS

Doctors call them "sick gains": the benefits of being ill. Crazy as it may sound, there are always benefits. Say you break your leg. That's painful and crippling, sure, but it also brings advantages. You receive more attention and sympathy. You get more value for money from your medical insurance. You're excused certain tasks. And you finally have time to read a book. So why should it be any different with problems affecting an organization? If the management team isn't functioning properly, that makes room for other people to set their own course. It creates new opportunities. Could this be why there are so many dysfunctional management teams?

■

## 45

RESISTANCE IS STRENGTH

Athletes are familiar with it, and so are army recruits: running through loose sand, climbing a dune at a constant speed, as if there's no resistance, or embarking on a long route march with a heavy pack. It's really not that different for organizations: resistance teaches you to find better arguments. To fly a kite, you need a headwind. Defiance is necessary for progress and change, in organizations just as anywhere else.

PROMISE ME, YOU'RE NOT FALLING IN LOVE...

## 46

TO GET AHEAD: STOP!

In the real world, we recognize it immediately: the paradoxical intervention. An inverse reaction that gets things moving, however stuck they may have seemed. Provocation as a remedy, to shake things up. Like when your girlfriend tells you she wants to dump you, and you say, "OK, great." The first thing she thinks is, "Uh-uh, I'm not gonna make it that easy for you!" Or a publisher who, after the deadline has already passed, suddenly says, "Let's just forget about it". There's a good chance I would have submitted an extra chapter. ■

## 47

DEFIANCE IS A DRIVER

A Boy Named Sue
My daddy left home when I was three
And he didn't leave much to ma and me
Just this old guitar and an empty bottle of booze
Now, I don't blame him cause he run and hid
But the meanest thing that he ever did
Was before he left, he went and named me "Sue"

Later in this famous song by Johnny Cash, the father explains why he called his son Sue. Because "this world is rough" and "I knew I wouldn't be there to help ya along", but with that name "you'd have to get tough or die".

## 48

REST CREATES MOVEMENT

What would a school do without recess? That's just as important as the curriculum, in the same way as rest is an essential part of an athlete's training. Sometimes you have to stand still in order to move ahead. It's no coincidence that some of the greatest discoveries have been made by people when they were doing absolutely nothing. Thomas Edison formulated new ideas while he was fishing and Woody Allen came up with his biggest box-office hits in the shower. What's outside the box belongs in the box. Always.

4'33"

John Cage

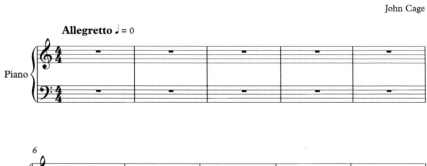

LET THE SILENCE SPEAK

Something amazing happened to me at the Spiritual Academy in Amsterdam. At irregular intervals, but at least once an hour, a bell rings in a minute's silence. Everyone stops what they're doing, says and does nothing for sixty seconds, and then carries on as if nothing has happened. A magical moment. Even during a meeting or the fiercest of debates. What seems to cost time actually generates it. A moment of silence so that you can focus on what's really important. Never has that been clearer to me than when listening to John Cage's famous 4'33". A composition in three movements in which not one note is played. I've attended several performances, and it never fails to impress me. ■

## 50

AUTHENTIC? THAT'S YOU

Authenticity is a hugely important aspect of persuasion.
Real people make an impression. Good actors know that better
than anyone, and so regard authenticity as a professional
skill. They perform, yet they remain themselves. Authentic
people are able to be themselves anywhere, at any time – in
other people's eyes, at least. But they're what matters.

DON'T MOTIVATE

Stop demotivating people, but don't motivate them.
That's the manager's most important task. Professional
employees are already motivated, and they regard their work
as an important means of personal development. Those
who are already motivated are only discouraged by attempts
to motivate them even more. If you push a donkey in the
direction it's already going, it will just come to a standstill. ■

## 52

DIVERSITY IS A RESOURCE

Nature's strength lies in her diversity. When it comes to survival, the prairie wins out over the English landscaped garden. The garden can't go a day without tending, making it extremely vulnerable. Anybody wanting to be equipped to face a complex environment and an unpredictable future should embrace diversity in every conceivable form. Monocultures like the financial sector may look more efficient, but that only makes them all the more vulnerable when adversity strikes.

## 53

DON'T INSPIRE, BUT BE INSPIRED

True professionals don't ask for motivation – they already have it. No, what they want is inspiration. And that's not an activity, not something you do – it's something you are. Inspirational people are people who are inspired themselves. People who put their all into their work, and who have no difficulty in imbuing others with confidence in theirs. Nothing is as inspiring as being trusted. Because people who don't trust themselves don't trust others. ■

## 54

KEEP IT SIMPLE, EXCEPT WHEN IT MATTERS

Conventional wisdom has it that clear, simple communication works. And that's true, at least when it comes to trivia. Where you have to be and at what time, for example, or in IKEA assembly instructions. With really important messages, though, simplification can be disastrous. Anyone who tries to tell people in a professional organization exactly what to do is bound to encounter resistance. "If you know so much about it, then do it yourself." To inspire people, give them space. Only then can they make the message their own and add something of themselves to it.

DARE
TO
ASK

One person's insurmountable challenge is another's stock
in trade. Most of us enjoy helping other people. In their
book Dare to Ask, Nils Roumen and Fanny Koerts show
just how far you can get by requesting assistance.
If you're prepared to help others, that also helps you. ■

DARE
TO
GIVE

"Give, and it shall be given unto you" (Luke 6:38).
Yes, even the Bible calls for what we call prosocial behavior.
Those willing to help are more likely to receive help when
they need it. What goes around, comes around. ∎

LET YOUR ACTIONS SPEAK

Actions speak louder than words – which often fall on deaf ears. Especially if they're unwelcome. Or gratuitous. Don't say "We have to do something" if you then do nothing. Announce that something is going to cost money and in many cases you won't get an answer. Until you send the bill. So rather than talking about what you're going to do, let your actions speak for themselves. Really, this is a plea for decisive transparency. Or what the German philosopher Jürgen Habermas calls "communicative action".

## 58

DON'T ARGUE

There are two kinds of resistance: major and minor. This may seem a straightforward observation, but it's one with massive repercussions. Minor resistance is an everyday occurrence. It's the kind of opposition you can ignore like a bump in the road. If the opposition grows, however, we have to come up with arguments to counter it. Problem solved. When the stakes are really high, though, resistance only increases as the case against it strengthens. In this situation, it's better to accept and respect the opposition. That disarms its resistance and creates room for dialogue.

## 59

DON'T BRAINSTORM

Brainstorming: it's the most widely used technique for generating ideas as a group. By agreeing that everyone can say what they want, more suggestions are put forward. At least, that's the theory.
But does it really work like that? No, not entirely. In fact, in this kind of process we tend to fall in line with the rest of the group. If we all came up with our own ideas separately, cumulatively that would probably produce more original and distinctive ones. This doesn't mean that brainstorming is never useful – for example, it can be a good way to get to know each other better, especially when you have to actually implement ideas that are already on the table.
But consider it more as a social occasion that also produces ideas. ∎

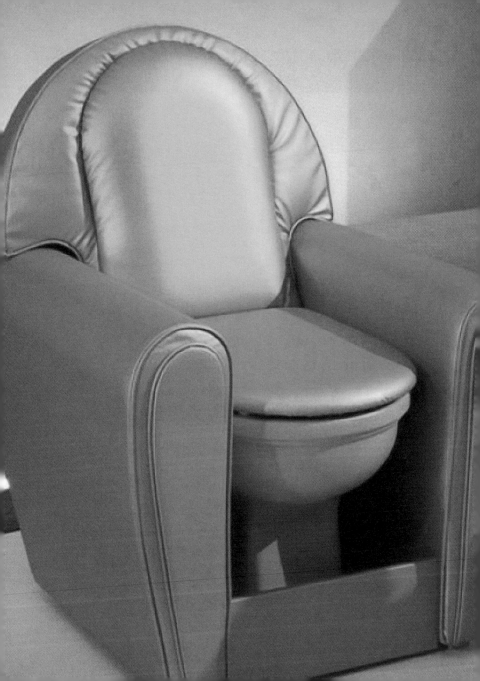

## 60

NO SOLUTION WITHOUT A PROBLEM

The management guru Henry Mintzberg likes to draw a distinction between successful managers and effective ones. Success is in the eye of the beholder – first and foremost, it's about perception. That doesn't necessarily make you ineffective, but you don't become an effective manager just by solving all kinds of problems, even though that's usually why people are appointed to management positions in the first place. You achieve effectiveness by making problems for employees in need of assistance. That's because problems necessitate solutions, in the same way as questions necessitate answers. The manager who just solves problems soon becomes the workplace handyman. ■

## 61

THE ORGANIZATION DOESN'T EXIST...

"Have you ever shaken the organization's hand?," my teacher
Edu Feltmann once asked. We seldom realize that an organization
is not a thing or a person, it's an idea, a mental construct.
That doesn't mean it's any less real, but it does make it easier to
change. If an organization is not functioning properly, you can change
it simply by adopting a different way of thinking. It's all in the mind. ■

## 62

...NOR DOES LEADERSHIP

Leadership is an ability endowed by others. Like beauty – and success – it's in the eye of the beholder. You're a leader because others see you as a leader. Leadership is not an objective reality, but a subjective observation. In his day, Eisenhower was widely regarded as a brilliant general but an average president. Since then, however, perceptions have changed and his role in the Second World War has attracted some criticism. Conversely, his presidency is now seen in a more positive light. Image plays a big role in leadership, and others largely determine your image. In a sense, it's the followers that decide who their leaders are. ■

63

THE
QUESTION
IS THE
ANSWER

If you want to learn something, you have to ask a question.
If you want to learn a lot, you have to ask a lot of questions.
A question always contains more than its answer.
That answer may satisfy your curiosity, but can also kill it. ■

## 64

THE RECURRING PROBLEM IS YOU

You can dismiss one divorce as bad luck, two as an unfortunate coincidence. But the third is a different story. Therein lies a message that's probably clear to those around you. At times like this, it might be a good idea to confide in friends. People who find themselves in the same predicament time and again are often the true cause of the problem. A person who's fired repeatedly should really ask himself why that is.

## 65

DON'T DECIDE WHAT'S ALREADY BEEN DECIDED

Some decisions emerge of their own accord, with no outside intervention required. My mentor told me that many of his fellow managers suffered from overinflated egos. They thought they had to decide everything, when in fact most things happen anyway and the decisions about them are taken naturally. Like a leaf floating down a river to the sea. If you decide what's already been decided, that generates resistance and brings ongoing processes to a standstill. ■

## 66

UNDERSTAND YOURSELF

Empathy is the ability to see things from another person's perspective. It's a trait we develop at an early age. At first sight it seems a peculiarly human phenomenon, but scientists have recently begun observing it in animals as well. Primatologist Frans de Waal has shown that apes can work together, solve conflicts and make up with each other after a dispute. Dolphins, too, help one another when they're in trouble.Seeing things as others do is a prerequisite for success, in business as much as in any other part of life. Understanding needs and satisfying them is not only the cornerstone of business, it's also at the heart of reciprocity in general. And understanding other people is a lot easier if you understand yourself. ■

## 67

THE SOLUTION IS THE PROBLEM

Managers often present themselves as the solution, which implies that there's a problem. Mary Parker Folett, a leading philosopher and management consultant in the nineteenth century, believed in a very different approach. Rather than looking at what was going wrong, she asked herself what was going right within organizations. And what did she find? Where no manager was involved, people followed their own instincts, drawing on their professional skills and common sense. In many cases, things only went wrong when a manager intervened and positioned himself or herself between the employee and the customer.

## 68

THE SITUATION IS HOPELESS
(but not serious)

This became a well-known saying in the Austro-Hungarian Empire as it teetered on the brink of collapse. The empire couldn't be saved, yet all its constituent countries survive to this day. Just as many of the companies that made up OGEM still exist. And far less of Fokker has disappeared than was feared when the aircraft manufacturer declared bankruptcy in 1996. Sometimes things just aren't as bad as they seem. The Dutch coal mines may all have closed, resulting in huge unemployment, but the modern industrial conglomerate DSM would never have existed if they hadn't. ∎

69

THE IRRELEVANT IS RELEVANT

When it comes to innovation, the irrelevant becomes relevant and the relevant irrelevant. What's at the edge now is going to come to the center. Managers usually want to know about the heart of the matter – true visionaries want to know what it's not about at all. ■

## 70

SCARCITY IS A BLESSING
(abundance a curse)

"Need teaches us to pray," we were told as kids. In other words, in times of trouble you learn to ask for help. Or be inventive. Perhaps the same applies to scarcity. It, too, can encourage invention. Vincent van Gogh once complained to his brother that he was so poor that yellows were almost the only paints he had left. ■

THE
FUTURE
IS
ALREADY
HERE

No-one can predict the future, except to say that it always
lurking just ahead of the present. For years self-employment
was a marginal phenomenon, but now everyone seems to
be a freelancer. The same goes for mobile phone, personal
trainers, network organizations, transgenders, you name it…
All existed long before the vast majority of us became aware
of them. As the management guru Gary Hamel once said,
"The future is already here – it's just not very evenly distributed." ■

Avis can't afford not to be nice.

Or not give you a new car like a lively, super-torque Ford, or not know a pastrami-on-rye place in Duluth. Why?

When you're not the biggest in rent a cars, you have to try harder.

We do. We're only No. 2.

## 72

THE LAW OF STIMULATIVE ARREARS

A small deficiency can deliver the greatest advantage – that's the Law of Stimulative Arrears. In cycle racing, second position is generally considered the best place to be during a sprint. The leader sets the pace and so assists the rider immediately behind him, who can see exactly what he has to do to win in the final seconds. Business schools rarely pay much attention to the advantages of being in second place, even though the examples are there for taking. Apple exploited them by being more user-friendly than the then-dominant Microsoft, and Avis came up with the slogan "We try harder" to promise its customers more than the market leader of the time. When it comes to overhauling organizations, there's an old adage: "'Never be first, but never be worse than second". The leader has to deal with the teething troubles, the number two can avoid them.

 # 73

THE LAW OF THE HANDICAP OF A HEAD START

If you have a lead now, you're only paving the way to fall behind later. That's the thinking behind the Law of the Handicap of a Head Start, also known as the dialectics of lead, originally formulated by the historian Jan Romein. In the 1930s he noticed that London was one of the last major world cities still lit by gas. That was because it had been the first to introduce street lighting, before the age of electricity. To upgrade to the new technology, it would have to discard one that was outdated but still functional. More recently, the pioneering Minitel system ended up hindering the advance of the more versatile laptop in France. ∎

## 74

THE OPPOSITE IS ALSO TRUE

That's actually the core message of this collection. And if the opposite is true, then that creates an endless series of possibilities. In business as in life, it's not the facts that count, but how you look at them. We owe this nugget of wisdom to the ancient Greek philosopher Epictetus. The world and all its possibilities change simply by looking at them in a different way – an approach Richard Branson has made his own. He breaks conventions by adopting different points of view and by simply doing things in ways that no-one else does.

## 75

THE BOOK IS OF ITS READER

After a public reading, the Dutch author Harry Mulisch was once asked about the meaning of a passage in one of his novels. His reply: "This is a strange misunderstanding. You clearly assume that it's my book. Yes, I wrote it. But you've read it. It's your book now. I'd be very interested to know the answer to your question!" Before the audience could come to terms with this answer, he went on, "There have been more versions of this book produced than I've written, because I've written only one." The auditorium still filled with a stunned silence, Mulisch continued. "You can never read a book twice. "Nobody's ever succeeded in doing that." Only later did I realize that he was echoing the Greek philosopher Heraclitus. ∎

CREDITS

#	
# 1	René Nuijens
# 2	Courtesy of Universal Studios Licensing LLC
# 3	China Photos/Getty Images
# 4	Rembrandt van Rijn/Rijksmuseum
# 5	Soyuz TMA spacecraft, National Aeronautics and Space Administration
# 6	Stephen J. Boitano/Getty Images
# 7	Joe Shere/mptvimages.com
# 8	Matt Jelonek/Getty Images
# 9	Sébastien Thibault/Anna Goodson Illustration Agency
# 10	Marcel Christ
# 11	Merlyn Severn/Getty Images
# 12	Alfred Stieglitz
# 13	Gerdjan van der Lugt
# 14	Charles Ommanney/Getty Images
# 15	Annelore van Herwijnen/www.annelore.nl
# 16	Sony Corporation
# 17	Martin Parr/Magnum/Hollandse Hoogte
# 18	Harry Pot
# 19	Rebecca Richardson
# 21	W. Eugene Smith/Getty Images
# 22	Kancho Flemming Jinzen
# 23	Yuri Gagarin/courtesy of René Nuijens
# 24	The Estate of Bas Jan Ader/Mary Sue Ader Andersen/The Artist Rights Society (ARS), New York/Courtesy of Meliksetian | Briggs, Los Angeles
# 25	Shepard Fairey/Obeygiant.com
# 26	Filip Dujardin - Untitled from series 'Fictions' - 2013/ courtesy Van der Mieden Gallery
# 27	Paul Baars Design
# 28	buro van Ons
# 29	Courtesy of the Marina Abramoviʹc Archives/Pictoright
# 30	Bernie Deyo
# 31	Jörg Dickmann/joergdickmann.com
# 32	John Downing/Getty Images
# 34	Mike Hollingshead (storm chaser)
# 36	Bundesarchiv
# 38	Rob Kroenert
# 41	Getty Images
# 42	Ullstein bild/Getty Images
# 43	Neil Fitzgerald
# 44	Reid, Geleijnse & Van Tol
# 45	Per Breiehagen/Getty Images

'Better roughly right
than exactly wrong.'

ACKNOWLEDGEMENTS

If it were a film, this collection would be described as an Aernoud Bourdrez & Peter Heykamp Production. True professionals both, they kept me focused on the task at hand whenever my attention wandered. Lion Versloot extended a helping hand, even though we hardly knew each other. A generous man. Joris Roovers helped keep the text comprehensible by putting himself in the reader's shoes when I was unable to. Muriel Janssen had no hesitation in offering me her beautiful photographs, and Ceciel Ex likewise with her art. Paul Baars, my neighbor on Frederiksplein in Amsterdam, provided valuable suggestions, as did Ilja Klink and Paul Hughes. Joost Steins Bisschop and Michiel Bicker Caarten reviewed an earlier version of the manuscript. Karin Jironet was a constant support. The English-language version was produced by Taalcentrum-VU. Mathieu Weggeman, Jo Houben, and my colleagues at De Nederlandse School were a source of inspiration. I remain solely and fully responsible for any errors in the text.

This collection is dedicated to my daughter and my son.
They were hardly out of my thoughts during its preparation.